UX Design Made Easy

Copyright 2021 by Paul Cundell

Harrogate, UK

www.uxdesignmadeeasy.com

All rights reserved.

First Printing, 2021.

All rights reserved. This book or any portion thereof may not be reproduced or used in any manner whatsoever without the express written permission of the publisher except for the use of brief quotations in a book review.

Limits of Liability / Disclaimer of Warranty

The authors and publisher of this book and the accompanying materials have used their best efforts in preparing this program. The authors and publisher make no representation or warranties with respect to the accuracy, applicability, fitness, or completeness of the contents of this program. They disclaim any warranties (expressed or implied), merchantability, or fitness for any particular purpose. The authors and publisher shall in no event be held liable for any loss or other damages, including but not limited to special, incidental, consequential, or other damages. As always, the advice of a competent legal, tax, accounting or other professional should be sought. The authors and publisher do not warrant the performance, effectiveness or applicability of any sites listed in this book. All links are for information purposes only and are not warranted for content, accuracy or any other implied or explicit purpose.

This manual contains material protected under International and Federal Copyright Laws and Treaties. Any unauthorized reprint or use of this material is prohibited.

"Design is the fundamental soul of a human-made creation that ends up expressing itself in successive outer layers of the product or service."

— Steve Jobs

Table of Contents

Chapter 1 – Introduction to UX Design

Chapter 2 – What Does a UX Designer Do?

Chapter 3 – UX Principle #1: User-Focused

Chapter 4 – UX Principle #2: Feedback

Chapter 5 – UX Principle #3: Digestibility

Chapter 6 – UX Principle #4: Clarity

Chapter 7 – UX Principle #5: Familiarity

Chapter 8 – UX Principle #6: Delight

Chapter 9 – Case Studies and Examples

Chapter 10 – The Future of UX Design

Chapter 11 – Putting It All Together

CHAPTER 1
INTRODUCTION TO UX DESIGN

Chapter 1 – Introduction to UX Design

Nowadays, many people automatically assume that user experience (UX) design can only be developed for websites, software, and tech products. Historically speaking, however, Don Norman of Apple coined the term to bridge the gap between the human interface and the usability of their products. For him, user experience goes beyond graphics or industrial design—it's also about how easy it is to learn and use the functions of a given product.

Over the years, his pioneering ideas about putting functionality over aesthetics have evolved into multiple areas of interest, such as Information Architecture and various methods of User Research. Moreover, UX design proves to be one of the key determining factors for the success or failure of companies—big or small.

Why?

Because a good UX design turns a product into something that people find useful, usable, and delightful. It ensures that the users will recognize the value of the product, and how that product can satisfy their needs and wants in life. As a result, having a good UX design can:

- Boost the company's ROI
  Did you know that for every dollar invested in UX, the company may expect up to $100 in return? Design-driven companies, such as Apple, Google, and Netflix, can attest to this based on the 2018 report of McKinsey & Company. These corporations earn higher revenues and increased shareholder returns by almost twice their competitors in their respective markets.

- Increase customer conversion rates
  UX tends to be one of the main deciding factors for users to choose a product over the others. Case in point, Apple smartphones are pricier compared to models with similar features and technical specifications. However, because of their focus on providing an excellent user experience as well as promoting the design of each new release, they manage time and again to convince a large portion of consumers to purchase their smartphones.

- Enhance customer retention rates
  By proving to customers that your product answers their needs through delightful solutions, you can gain and build their trust and loyalty to your brand. Rewards apps, for example, can be an effective way to encourage customers to keep choosing you despite the other new and existing options in the market.

- Reduce operational costs
  Because of the rigorous testing requirements of the standard UX design process, companies may be able to save on operational costs for processing and resolving customer complaints later on when the product has been launched.

> "Because a good UX design turns a product into something that people find useful, usable, and delightful."

Given these, UX design does not only benefit the users themselves, but also those who are willing to invest time, energy, and resources for its development. But how exactly can a useful, usable, and delightful product be created?

It's easier said than done, as you will learn later on in this book.

The succeeding chapters will show you the various stages that UX designers go through before a product with excellent UX design can be launched. We'll also tackle the skills and qualities that you must possess to excel in this field.

Since UX design is guided by six principles, a large portion of this book is dedicated to discussing each design, and how they should be reflected in different aspects of the design process and the product itself.

To better illustrate why everyone should pay more attention to UX design, I'll share with you selected case studies featuring companies that have successfully satisfied the needs and wants of their customers through carefully designed UX. By the end of this book, you will get a better grasp of whether or not UX design is something you wish to pursue as a passion and career.

CHAPTER 2

WHAT DOES A UX DESIGNER DO?

Chapter 2 – What Does a UX Designer Do?

Excellent UX designers genuinely care about how other people think and feel about their products. They don't just observe for the sake of obtaining data. Their minds always seek innovative ways to resolve any issues that people encounter while using the product. For them, maximizing the usefulness of the product goes hand-in-hand with ensuring that it will also delight the users.

What does it take to excel in this field though?

Here are the six core skills and qualities that you should acquire and master if you're interested in taking this career path:

- <u>Technical Skills</u>
  Here's the thing: UX designers are not synonymous with developers and programmers. They don't need to master coding or be proficient at using programming tools to translate what the users need and want out of the product.

  However, UX designers who excel in this field can speak the same language and understand the mindset of the technical experts. Being disconnected from the technical aspects of the product will make the UX design process a lot harder. They need to feel comfortable about discussing their ideas with developers to learn how things work, and how issues can be resolved.

  UX designers should take the time to use prototyping tools and other similar programs, too. By doing so, they would have a better understanding of the development process, as well as increase their knowledge of basic programming language.

- <u>High Empathy</u>
  Having the ability to put yourself in someone's shoes and see from their point of view enables UX designers to create solutions that are well-fitted to the target users of the product. Though the level of empathy varies from one person to another, you can build this skill over time through observation and mindfulness exercises.

  Pay attention to the day-to-day life experiences of other people. Take note of their reactions to certain situations. Spend time absorbing how other products or apps are designed, and then reflect on how they made you feel. After all, empathy stems from having an awareness of your thoughts and feelings. I suggest exercises such as yoga, meditation, or journaling to get in touch with your inner self, and in the same process, increase your ability to empathize with other people.

- <u>Effective Communication Skills</u>
  Being able to communicate well is necessary for every step in the UX design process. You need it to explain your ideas and comments about others' suggestions. Research work involving target users can only be successfully done if the designer can ask the right questions and listen well to their feedback. Presenting prototypes and test results also requires a high degree of communication skills.

  Within the team, good communication among the members must be maintained since different kinds of opinions would likely be given to one another at various points of the process. UX designers should be able to receive opinions—especially negative but constructive ones—without being offended or disheartened.

- Enthusiasm Towards Learning
  The field of UX design continually develops so what you know today might no longer be applicable by the next day. As such, excellent UX designers feel a strong desire to discover and explore new things.

  Nowadays, there are plenty of ways to learn continuously. It just depends on how much time and effort you can commit to this initiative. For example, some UX designers join online courses and webinars that they can engage in after work hours. Many enjoy reading educational blog posts and podcasts about topics that they are interested in. If you prefer something that involves meeting new people and learning something from them, look into local social events that will also help you build your professional network as a UX designer.

- Strong Critical Thinking
  As you will learn later on in this book, one of the key elements of a good UX design is derived from having the ability to ask why. UX designers don't hesitate to challenge the ideas and concepts presented to them. They know that understanding how things work usually involves probing into the system and connections of every design element.

  Critical thinking also helps UX designers to come up with outside-the-box solutions. By having a good grasp of what needs to be done, they can analyze how the product should be designed to elicit the desired reactions from the target users.

- Self-Confidence
  Many parts of the UX design process require the designers to be intuitive. Listening to your guts take

courage so it's necessary for professionals in this field to be confident about their ideas and to stand by them if their guts are telling them to just go for it. After all, human interactions cannot be completely described using statistical data only.

Of course, UX designers rely heavily on test results to move forward with their projects. However, there is nothing wrong with trusting your instincts as a designer—as long as you are willing to own up to your mistakes and make up for them with the new things that you have learned.

As you can see, these six skills and qualities can be developed and enhanced over time as you gain more experience in UX design. Remember that each one is necessary to successfully carry out the UX design process, which has the following 5 key stages:

A. <u>Planning</u>
The process begins with a kickoff meeting attended by everyone involved in the project. At this point, the team should:
- Deliberate about the purpose, concept, and value proposition of the product
- Identify what is needed to make the project a success
- Conduct risk assessment for the project
- Set SMART goals (specific, measurable, achievable, realistic, and time-bound)
- Assign deliverables with corresponding timelines

B. <u>Researching</u>
Since UX design is user-focused, research must be conducted to better understand the users' needs and wants. Skipping this stage will likely lead to a product

that is useless, unusable, or unpleasant for the end-users.

Different approaches may be taken to gather the necessary information—for example:
- Focus Group
  This involves asking a group of potential users about their thoughts and feelings about a product or design.
- Survey
  To do this, a questionnaire must be prepared and administered to the target users. Surveys can also be used to objectively assess the usability of a product through the System Usability Scale.
- User Interview
  One-on-one interviews with potential users can be an effective way to understand their needs, problems, and expectations about a particular product.
- User Persona
  Creating a realistic user persona can help designers recognize and analyze the key characteristics of the target users. This does not only include demographic information but also the personality, motivations, and the common issues faced by the users that the persona is representing.

> "How do I explain what I do at a party? The short version is that I say I humanize technology."
>
> Fred Beecher of "The

C. Designing

This stage involves a series of activities to create a prototype of the desired UX design. It starts with a minimalistic sketch of the design to consolidate ideas and refine the proposed design.

Wireframes of the design ideas will then be prepared to define the basic elements and layout. The goal is to gather the initial feedback of other people involved about the proposed design so that revisions can still be made before proceeding to the more time-consuming parts of this stage.

The information architecture (IA) of the design must also be defined to prevent users from experiencing information overload when engaging with the product. Most UX designers rely on either the tree testing technique or card sorting to figure out how to make the design easier to absorb and navigate.

Paying attention to the user flow is essential, too. This entails mapping the different interactions that users would likely make with the product. By doing so, the designer will have a better idea of how the user must be guided to achieve what they want out of the product.

Once all the necessary elements and information have been gathered, a prototype will be created to

> **Take Note!**
>
> The best kind of user flow map feels like a delightful conversation rather than a cold, robotic account of the user's interactions with the interface. While the latter is still going to be useful, an organic user flow would enhance the effectiveness and quality of the design.

showcase how the actual design is going to look based on the ideas and feedback that the designers have received so far. In general, multiple prototypes may be done throughout the UX design process, but the level of implementation varies depending on the intended use of the prototype:

- Low-Fidelity Prototype
  Use this during the earlier parts of the process to encourage creative or innovative suggestions. A low-fidelity prototype contains the basic design and content elements but no information about user interactions. Since this is typically done on paper only, it's a low-cost UX design tool that can be created quickly.

- Mid-Fidelity Prototype
  User interactions are best tested through this prototype. This bears a closer resemblance to what the final product would be like, but its functionality is limited.

- High-Fidelity Prototype
  Designers who are going to test the usability of the product create a prototype that almost looks like how the final design will be in terms of appearance and function. This type can also be used to obtain the final approval for the design. Because it must contain every design and content element, high-fidelity prototypes tend to be expensive and time-consuming.

D. Testing
Testing the design does not only provide a measure of how easy the product can be used; It also ensures that no issues will be overlooked before the launch. Usability

should be tested against previous versions of the design, as well as against competitors. Summative testing—wherein at least 20 users test the product for its reliability—must also be conducted before launching. Other common types of testing include:

- **User Testing**
  This involves observing a group of target users interacting with the product.

- **Beta Launch**
  Known also as a limited release, this allows designers to obtain data from actual users about any remaining issues with the product. As such, solutions can be developed and applied before the product is fully launched to the market.

Internal testing is critical for the UX design process, too. The internal team should test every aspect of the product and then duly communicate all significant observations to everyone involved.

E. <u>Analyzing</u>
Test results should be analyzed to highlight key points and issues that must be considered before proceeding to the next step. In case major issues have been found, the team should work on solutions based on how big the impact they could have on the users. Iterations are also necessary to determine if the proposed solutions would effectively address the issues.

Once the analysis of the test results indicates that the product has optimal usefulness, usability, and delightfulness, the team can move forward and launch the product. While designs aren't going to be perfect no matter how rigorous every stage had been, the standard UX design process significantly increases the effectiveness and success rate of the design.

UX designers should continue to analyze the results of their hard work after the product has been launched. To do so, they ask questions such as:

- What are the users' perceptions of the product?
- How are the users responding to the product?
- Did the users think that the product has addressed their needs or resolved their issues?
- How can the product be further improved?

It's important to reflect about how the journey that the team has taken. This involves answering questions like:

- Which stages of the design process went well? Why?
- Which stages of the design process were particularly challenging? Why?
- What lessons can be taken away from this project and should be applied to the next ones?

Throughout this entire process, the designer must keep in mind the six core principles of UX design. Each principle is rooted in various psychological theories that influence how the app should be designed and how the users will perceive the product. We'll discuss further these six principles and their applications in the succeeding chapters.

CHAPTER 3

UX PRINCIPLE #1: USER-FOCUSED

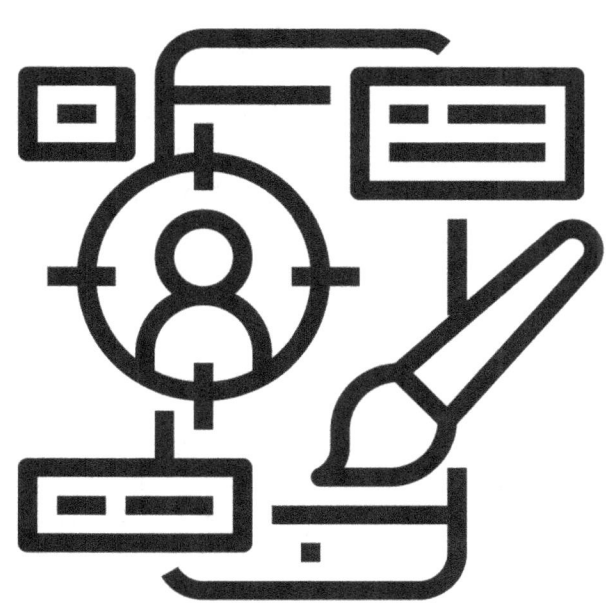

You may have excellent personal tastes, but as a UX designer, they don't matter as much as the preferences of the end-users. Of course, you're free to express yourself in your work. However, the focal point of your design should always be your target audience.

To abide by this UX principle, take the time to reach out to the users and ask them the right questions. Assuming that you know what they like and want can keep you from producing an appealing, engaging, and productive experience for them. As discussed in the previous chapter, some of the most commonly used research methods in UX design are focus groups, surveys, user interviews, and user personas.

Let's go over how a typical user interview goes to better illustrate how your design can be user-focused.

First, get to know the user's background. Start by throwing some casual questions like, "How are you feeling today?" or "What was your commute like going here?"

Once the interviewee has started settling in, move on to questions that will shed light on their background. Inquire about their current needs in life, too. By doing so, you will be able to form a better idea of what type of person you're going to deal with.

Remember!

Disregard your assumptions about the users. Maintain an open mind, and take pleasure in discovering the quirks and nuances that they may have in relation to the product that you're designing.

Don't forget to keep your eye on the goal of the user interview though. Listen well to what the users have to say, but stay focused on what you have set out to do in the first place.

A quick tip: Reassure them that everything they share with you will be kept confidential and that they don't need to answer every question if they don't feel comfortable about it.

Take for example the user interview conducted by Anna, a UX designer for a new US-based ride-hailing app. The initial market research indicates that the target market resides in central business areas.

By interviewing a small group of potential app users, Anna learned that these individuals commute frequently for personal and work reasons. While they wished to purchase a vehicle of their own, their incomes, savings, or even credit scores aren't enough to push through with this investment.

Moreover, many of the interviewees have noticed that insufficient parking space continues to be a perennial issue in their respective areas. Anna also noted that the users of the app are young professionals whose needs cannot be met because of various factors, such as financial constraints and poor city planning.

From this point, Anna narrowed down to the expectations of the users for a ride-hailing app. Which of their needs would be satisfied by the app? What goals do they have in mind when they use the app? By seeking the answers to questions like these, Anna may find the connections between the user and the app. Consequently, her UX design could help turn the users' expectations into a reality.

During the latter end of the user interview, Anna applied the 5 Whys technique to gain further insights into how the app design should be. Check out the exchange below between Anna and Charles, one of the interviewees.

>Anna: Why do you want to use a ride-hailing app?

>Charles: To go to work.
>
>Anna: Why do you need to go to work?
>
>Charles: So that I can keep earning money.
>
>Anna: Can you share with me why you want to earn money?
>
>Charles: To pay off my bills and save some for the future.
>
>Anna: Why is that?
>
>Charles: I want to become more financially independent.
>
>Anna: Why are you setting such a goal for yourself?
>
>Charles: So that I can go after my other dreams in life.

As you can see, the 5 Whys technique allowed Anna to discover the deeper needs of the user. Based on the gathered information, the design of the ride-hailing app should cater to career-focused individuals who are looking for cheaper alternatives so they can save or spend their hard-earned money on other important things in their life.

One probable design solution is to open a ride-sharing option for those who are heading towards the same area. Another idea is to enable cash-back for users who pay for their rides through the in-app payment mode.

But what if you don't have the opportunity to conduct user interviews directly with the target audience?

I recommend either joining the online community discussions that those users take part in, or consuming the same kind of media content—such as movies or TV shows—as they do. Pay careful attention to commonly exhibited traits and tendencies of individuals you are observing.

Then, use that information to create user personas to serve as representatives for the types of users that will likely use the product. Like actual people, user personas should serve as your guide in designing solutions that will fulfill the needs and wants of the end-users.

CHAPTER 4

UX PRINCIPLE #2: FEEDBACK

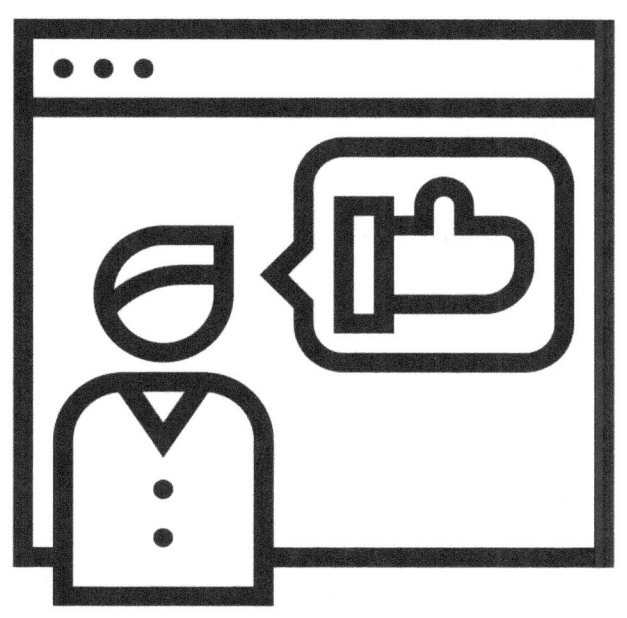

Chapter 4 – UX Principle #2: Feedback

Ever had a conversation with someone who didn't respond to what you were saying—not a word or even just a facial expression? Aside from being awkward, the lack of feedback also causes frustration and confusion. Should you keep going until something finally happens? Or is there anything else that must be done to get a reaction?

Much like conversations, feedback from an interface is essential for users. The product is designed for human interactions. Therefore, a response from the interface should be given to acknowledge the user and show that their interactions with the product are being processed.

Imagine a user tapping a button to proceed with your registration on a social media platform. How would they know that all the required information has been provided? A simple but effective means can be the appearance of a green checkmark followed by the standard hourglass loading icon. Seeing this on their screen gives the impression that everything is going smoothly so far.

Now, what if that user tapped the button and nothing happened? Not a change in color of the button or even a textbox indicating that the registration is being processed.

More often than not, the user will assume that the site isn't working. They might also check if their device is still connected to the Internet. If there seems to be no issue on their end, the user may start thinking that the platform isn't reliable, and thus cannot be easily trusted with their personal information.

As you can see, feedback is necessary—not only to keep the users interacting with the product in that particular moment—but also to build their trust and loyalty to the brand or company.

How can UX designers comply with this principle?

In general, there are three ways to respond to the users:

- A. Visual Feedback
  As described in the example above, visual feedback is as simple as assigning colors, symbols, or other images to communicate certain messages to the user. It can also be accompanied by actual words in case the changes in color or shape are not obvious or universally recognized.

- B. Audio Feedback
  Before voice commands have become a thing, audio feedback was usually just brief sound effects to go along with certain input or changes in the interface. For example, when the user has made an error, a jarring sound clip will play out to call the user's attention. Computer operating systems, like Windows and macOS, welcome users with a pleasant sound to indicate that sign-in has been successful or that the device has booted up.

  Voice commands have been developed to give more human-like responses these days. They don't sound cold and perfunctory anymore. Instead, Apple's Siri and Amazon's Alexa reply to users' requests and commands in a conversational manner. Some even noted that they have distinct personalities that shine through the choice of words and tone of voice.

- C. Haptic Feedback
  Though slick touchscreens have become the norm for many tech products nowadays, a lot of people continue to appreciate having a physical button to press when they activate a particular function or input information.

Take for example a computer keyboard. Though the technology for digital or projected keyboards is now available, manufacturers still develop and release desktop computers and laptop models that feature the standard physical keyboard design.

Sure, alterations to the design have been made over the years—for example, Apple's ill-received butterfly keyboard. However, the basic premise of providing a way for users to type in information through physical keys persists up to this day. After all, it allows people to find the right keys even without looking down at their fingers frequently.

Observe how websites and software give feedback to their users. As mentioned earlier, certain types of feedback are more appropriated for a particular application. Feel free to use more than one type though if you think it's necessary for the design. The important thing is to make the users feel heard and valued while they are using the product.

"As you can see, feedback is essential—not only to keep the users interacting with the product in that particular moment—but also to build their trust and loyalty to the company providing the product."

CHAPTER 5

UX PRINCIPLE #3: DIGESTIBILITY

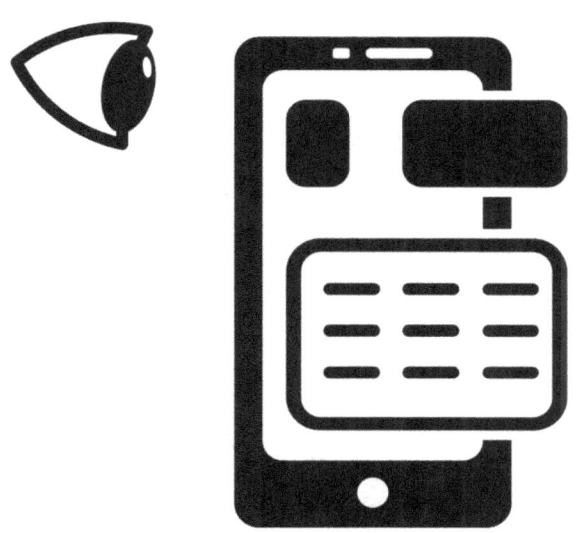

Many people feel dread upon seeing a wall of text on their screens. The mere sight drives away their interest, even if the information contained is useful or necessary to the reader.

Similarly, an app that sends out too many notifications in a day has a high chance of being muted by the users. After all, our attention is being pulled in multiple different directions at any given time, so those frequent notifications will likely become a burden instead of being helpful reminders or exciting announcements.

Why is this so?

The human brain isn't exactly thrilled to process a lot of information in a short period because it costs too much energy. Since we don't have limitless energy, forcing the brain to go through this leads to information overload—a psychological phenomenon that reduces one's capacity to make logical and reasonable decisions.

Inexperienced UX designers often make the mistake of cramming too much information because they don't examine well and deeply enough the needs of the users. If the person wishes to sign up for a new gaming account, they won't likely appreciate being asked to fill out an unusually long questionnaire or form with too many input fields.

People want to try out the game as soon as possible! Therefore, besides the basic information like username, email address, and password, input fields for other important details can be placed in their account settings instead.

How can UX designers make their work more digestible then?

Solutions for this mostly stem from the psychological theory about working memory, as explained by Prof. George Miller of Princeton University. According to his research, the brain remembers information in chunks. On average, a person's working memory can hold around 5 to 9 chunks of information at a particular instance.

To better illustrate this concept, take a look at the two sets of phone numbers below:

    Example 1: +1-910-333-8304

    Example 2: 19103338304

Of the two examples, which one do you think is more memorable for you? Most people would answer Example 1 because the digits are divided into smaller units that are within the average capacity of a person's working memory. Moreover, this arrangement makes the design more appropriate for skimming.

What does "skimming" mean?

People don't look and read carefully everything they see, especially on apps and websites. Instead, they scan down the screen to see if anything is interesting or valuable for them. Only then would they pay more careful attention to what is being presented to them. This means that designers should evaluate which content would not only be attention-grabbing but also informative and digestible within a brief period.

Given these, UX designers should ensure that their interfaces are broken down into smaller chunks. Let me share with you some valuable tips on how this can be done:

- For Text Content

- Write short paragraphs only—around 2 to 4 sentences per paragraph.
- Use white space to separate one paragraph from the next.
- Use headers and sub-headers that stand out from the rest of the text. For example, you can assign a larger font size for the header while the sub-headers are of the same size as the body but in bold typeface.
- Use bullets, numbers, or letters for lists or to show the hierarchy of information.
- Break strings of letters or numbers using symbols such as a hyphen, a pair of parentheses, or a slash.

- For Multimedia Content

    - Apply the law of proximity—a psychological concept that demonstrates how easy it is to absorb content if related things are in alignment or placed near each other.
    - Use white space, horizontal lines, or different background colors to distinguish one content from another.
    - Long videos or graphics can be divided into shorter clips according to the topic or segment.

- For Long Forms

    - Divide a long questionnaire or form into steps to make it look less intimidating.
    - Show the progress the user has made in filling out the form by indicating the number of questions or steps left.
    - For input fields that require a series of digits or codes, set the field to automatically place the

designated breaker—like a forward slash for dates or hyphen for credit card numbers—so that the user won't have to type them in themselves.

Presenting information in chunks makes the design more digestible for the users. Highlight the important and interesting aspects of your design, and define the relationships among its elements. By doing so, users will find your design to be both useful and memorable.

CHAPTER 6

UX PRINCIPLE #4: CLARITY

Chapter 6 – UX Principle #4: Clarity

A good UX design reflects the purpose and intention of the product. It doesn't trick the users into assuming that the product is meant to meet their needs or solve their issues. Instead, the design clarifies what the users can get out of the product right away.

For example, a company selling cellphone cases should specify in clear terms for which models would each case be suitable. If the case also protects the phone from being damaged due to a fall, then the product description must also highlight this feature.

> **What are Double Negatives?**
>
> It's the usage of a negative word—such as "No"—in settings related to actions like canceling a selection or terminating a process.

Other than answering the questions that the shoppers will likely have even before they were asked, stating the clear specifications of the product will also help potential buyers to understand the value and usefulness of the product that you're trying to sell.

The principle of clarity in UX design should also be expressed every step of the way. If you're encouraging users to subscribe to the company's newsletter, they should be informed about the kinds of content they will receive by doing so. Let them know how frequently the newsletters will be sent to their emails, too.

This design principle is even more important when it comes to the purchase of the product. Since you'd be asking for sensitive information such as the name of the buyer, their address, and credit card information, you have to find a way to reassure them that those details will be kept secured and will only be used to process their orders.

Ever tried registering for an app or service just because of its free trial period? Giving this option to interested users is a common sales and marketing strategy these days. However, more often than not, users are required to provide their credit card information during the trial registration, even if no payment would be demanded yet.

Understandably, many don't feel comfortable giving out such information right away. It might seem like they are being tricked into paying for something that they aren't certain yet if it's a good product or if it is helpful for them.

Another turn-off for users, in this case, is the lack of advance notice that they need to have a credit card just to avail of the free trial. Even if they want to try out the product, designers can't assume that everyone has a credit card these days. Clarifying this requirement right from the start will save the users some time and keep them from feeling bad about the product.

So, how can you express the principle of clarity through your UX design?

Did you know that...

Almost 50% of online shoppers don't continue browsing a website if they couldn't understand its purpose right away. These shoppers also dislike e-commerce websites that fail to provide their contact information.

Too many animated ads and confusing website navigation have also been mentioned as frequent causes for the poor performance of online shopping platforms.

In general, it all boils down to the choice of words.

Be careful about the words you select to inform or explain to the user what is going on with the product or interface. For example, UX designers avoid using double negatives when asking users to confirm their actions.

Facebook made this blunder a few years ago with their confirmation textbox that appeared when the users wanted to cancel the upload of photos to their account. In the textbox that asked if the user was certain about canceling the upload, the button options provided were either "Confirm" or "Cancel".

Now, if it's your first time using this option, what do you think will the "Cancel" button of the textbox does? Would selecting that option cause the cancellation of the upload? Or would it take back the user's prompt to cancel the upload?

Because of the double negatives, many users tend to become confused and ended up selecting the wrong button. As a result, they will have to do the process all over again, which could then lead to frustration about the interface.

Aside from the choice of words, clarity can also be achieved through the Golden Rule. Inform your users how you want to be informed. Explain how things work like how you want others to explain things for you.

Don't expect everyone to understand right away what you mean. In turn, users will not abandon your product because they can't figure out what you're trying to say to them.

CHAPTER 7

UX PRINCIPLE #5: FAMILIARITY

Chapter 7 – UX Principle #5: Familiarity

While designers should look for ways to make their works unique and original, it's not imperative for everyone to completely change things up every time a new design is needed.

If an unfamiliar interface failed to make a connection with the user, then everything else will be rendered useless. The user will likely look for alternatives that don't require them to relearn a lot of things even if the product's features are inherently better than what others offer.

In the field of UX, achieving familiarity with the design can be done in various ways. Let's go over each one to better understand this UX design principle:

A. Exposure

This principle is based on the psychological concept called the mere-exposure effect. The brain prefers something already familiar due to prior exposure.

If a design bears a resemblance to products or interfaces that the person has already seen or used before, then the brain would require less energy to interact with the said design. Absorption of the content will also be faster since the brain can focus on what matters rather than exert additional effort on getting used to the new design.

Take for example the icon for the Recycle Bin in Windows OS. It looks like a drawing of a trash bin with the standard symbol for "recycle". Without even reading the icon name, many people would assume that it's related to files that have been deleted. Because of the symbol, they will also quickly understand its purpose:

Temporary storage for deleted files that may still be brought back and reused as long as the user has not yet purged the recycle bin.

B. Consistency

Familiarity in UX design can also be reflected through consistency. For instance, Apple smartphones and tablets have similar design elements both in terms of form, user interface, and processes.

Transferring data from one device to another is also made simpler and faster. Such strategies allow the brand to convince its existing phone users to purchase an iPad in case they are considering getting a tablet as well and vice versa.

Shopping websites also tend to apply the same UX design for their checkout processes. After the person has finished browsing through the goods and added the ones they want to purchase in the online cart, the standard checkout process requires the shopper to fill in their name, shipping address, billing address, and payment information. Businesses want to make this process as easy and quick as possible because if it's overly complicated, then the shopper might get frustrated and change their mind about the purchase.

C. Thematic Style

Another way to increase the familiarity of the design is by following a thematic style for the design elements. Again, the goal here is to minimize the cognitive resources needed by the user to interact with your product. By applying a thematic style that remains consistent throughout the design, you can make the experience more intuitive for the user.

Take note that this UX design principle does not completely hinder the flow of new ideas and concepts. Instead, it encourages designers to use existing designs as reference materials and jump-off points for their solutions and innovations.

Over time, the newest iteration of the product may turn out to be quite different from the first generation. That's acceptable for most users, provided that the evolution of the product has occurred gradually. They have had enough time to become familiar with the changes and embrace the direction of the brand.

CHAPTER 8

UX PRINCIPLE #6: DELIGHT

Chapter 8 – UX Principle #6: Delight

A product that is both useful and usable won't still make quite an impression among users if they don't find it delightful, too.

Think of a chocolate cake without frosting. While it's still tasty and filling, most people would likely not enjoy it as much as they would have if it is covered with rich chocolate frosting. However, don't focus on the frosting alone! Yes, kids tend to love that idea, but the average person looks forward to eating the cake as well.

The key, therefore, is achieving a balance among the three qualities of a good UX design. After having thought of how to optimize the usefulness and usability of your product, you need to figure out how to make the users smile and feel delighted by what you have to offer.

> **Fun Fact!**
>
> The human brain processes images 60,000 times faster than texts. That's why many UX designers who aim to quickly grab the attention of users go for interesting graphics rather than an informative text box.

How can your design delight the users?

A large portion of UX designers rely on these four strategies:

>Strategy #1: <u>Images</u>
>
>The right image can encapsulate the entire message that the designers want to convey about the product. As such, this is an effective way to connect better and faster with the users.

Images may either be photographs or illustrations. Don't simply rely on the first batch of generic stock images that you see, though. If you can't hand-draw illustrations or take original photos, spend time going through the available options, and select the ones that stand out from the crowd.

Remember that the chosen images should not be too distracting. The product itself must still shine and remain functional. Otherwise, the users will just take one look at your design and then move on to something else that can satisfy their needs and wants.

Strategy #2: Animation

Much like images, animation can help UX designers tell a story more creatively. Some animations can also improve the functionality of the product—for example, when it is used to provide feedback to the user's input.

However, animations require careful selection and application. Inexperienced designers tend to go over the top with this strategy. As such, rather than enhancing the interface, the animations can distract the users from what they want to do with the product.

Moreover, too many animations can slow down a website or software. Longer loading times might turn away users due to frustration or impatience.

Strategy #3: Witty Copywriting

A word of caution first: Apply this strategy only if the branding of the product or company goes well with a humorous tone. Otherwise, it may cause users to assume that the product isn't what they are looking for, or that the company is insincere about its purpose.

When done correctly, however, witty copywriting can be quite delightful to users. Aside from giving fun or quirky impression, it can be used to lighten up situations wherein the user might feel frustrated, such as errors or lags in the website. Cleverness may also be appreciated if the process requires the user to wait for feedback about their query.

Remember that the UX design principle of clarity must be observed even when you're trying to delight your users with a quick joke or two. Pay attention to how users react to the copywriting during the testing phase to gauge how effective this strategy will be, not only in getting a smile from the users but also in encouraging them to keep using the product.

Strategy #4: <u>Ease of Use</u>

Creative solutions aren't all that great if they would only end up complicating the process for the user. Sometimes, the more ideas you cram into the design, the less appealing it becomes.

Rather than putting all your time into thinking of how to add more visuals or text to the interface, sometimes the best course of action is to find a way to simplify things as much as possible. Just think about it. How delightful would a money transfer app be if it's quick and easy to learn, while still being a secured and convenient way to send money to your friend or a vendor?

That's why many UX designers consider this strategy to be the ultimate form of delight. The product is so easy to use that people don't think of it as a mere product. Instead, it becomes an essential part of their daily life.

To effectively use these strategies, beginners should observe how successful websites and apps apply them. Better yet, study some companies with similar branding as your project. Pay attention to how they apply the strategies, and take note of which ones would likely work well when implemented on your UX design.

As a head-start, the next chapter contains several case studies of brands and companies that have made the most out of the potential that UX can bring to their products. Go over each example and learn more about how the six design principles we have discussed in this book are applied in the real world.

CHAPTER 9

CASE STUDIES AND EXAMPLES

Chapter 9 – Case Studies and Examples

An excellent UX design isn't just pleasing to the eyes. Instead, it reflects the careful research, planning, and testing conducted by the team to form true connections between people and their product.

To show you how this looks, let me share with you seven awe-inspiring case studies and examples of UX design done right.

1. **Airbnb**

    This company truly believes in how UX design can unlock the full potential of its business. Famous for creating a font of their own, Airbnb has taken the six principles seriously and applied them to create a clear, responsive, and minimalist UX design for both their website and app.

    Given the large amount of information that users expect from a booking site, Airbnb did extremely well in minimizing clutter and pushing to the forefront the bits of information that the users would want to see.

    Airbnb designers have also managed to understand deeply the behavior of their users. As such, they were able to create an interface that can predict how users will react and what their next actions will probably be. Through this, they boosted not only the usefulness of the platform but also significantly increased its usability for their diverse user groups.

    In terms of visual appeal, Airbnb made it a point to present numerous options to its users without overwhelming them to the point of completely abandoning the page. They made cards to showcase what they have to offer to travelers and to provide all the necessary information that may be required to secure a reservation.

That said, a minimalist UX design has been proven to be a powerful way to ensure smooth processes, boost usability, and ensure the readability of the content.

2. Amazon Kindle

This reading app is one of the first to enter the market. Its lasting power can be attributed to a large number of contributors and incredibly diverse readers. However, you can't deny that Kindle's accessible UX design has also played a critical role in encouraging people to keep using the app despite the numerous alternatives available nowadays.

The Kindle designers have aimed to create an interface that can cater to the needs of everyone. With that in mind, they developed new features that enable different kinds of readers to adjust the app to suit their needs and preferences.

For example, those with light to moderate visual impairments are free to use the features that make reading not only possible but also comfortable. People who prefer to have someone read the content out loud have the option to use the assistive feature called VoiceOver. Such UX design decisions attract the attention of book lovers, as well as those who want to take up reading as a hobby.

3. **Calm**

   Sometimes, a delightful user experience does not have to be fun, exciting, or quirky. As in the case of the Calm app, their UX designers have captured the true essence of the app—relaxation—and then communicated them well to the users.

   When you first use the app, a series of questions will greet you to gauge your needs and expectations. Through the right choice of words and colors, the questionnaire doesn't ruin the impression that Calm only wants to establish a genuine but carefree relationship with its user.

   Furthermore, the questions at the start simplify the setup process and require only minimal cognitive effort from the user. After all, people who wish to use apps like this wouldn't be so keen to use something too complicated for them. Calm's straightforward interface sends a clear message that it will deliver a relaxing and comfortable experience to the users.

4. **Duolingo**

   This educational app has contributed a lot in changing the way people learn and master new languages. Its design allows users to go at their own pace using their device and without having to rely on the supervision of another person.

   The restrictions imposed due to the pandemic heightened further Duolingo's popularity, but what exactly makes it stand out from several other language-focused apps?

According to a survey among its users, what they appreciate the most is how Duolingo breaks down the learning process and topics into more manageable chunks. Their interface simplifies the experience too, thereby allowing users to concentrate on memorizing new vocabulary and understanding how to use those new words correctly.

Duolingo designers made the right call in asking questions one by one rather than expecting users to answer a series of questions in just a single form. As a result, users don't feel overwhelmed, and they feel a sense of accomplishment through the immediate feedback given once they have inputted their answers.

5. **Instagram**

    Ever find yourself casually scrolling through Instagram only to realize that you've been at it for several minutes—or even hours—already? Lots of people did, and most likely continue to do so.

    What Instagram got right about the UX design is its dedication to visual efficiency. Given its nature as an image and video sharing platform, there's a high risk of becoming too overwhelming for users. That's why the designers decided to reduce visual noise as much as possible.

    Take a look at its interface, and observe how the focus is mostly on the content shared by the users in their accounts. Don't assume that the app achieved this degree of visual efficiency by sacrificing function, however.

Its UX designers just figured out a layout wherein they can minimize the appearance of the other features and settings, while keeping them accessible to the user at any time.

Note how Instagram relies on familiar icons on their interface, too. For example, the camera icon is unobtrusive but it tells right away to the user what it is in case they ever feel the need to take photos or videos to share on the app.

All in all, Instagram managed to make the most of their screen space to delight the users who just want to see and engage with interesting content in their feed.

6. Nike

The online store of Nike shows how UX design principles can boost revenues. If you would take a look at their website, you will notice how the designers opt to apply the theory of proximity to convert the interest of shoppers into actual sales.

Try selecting a pair of shoes from their online selection. Doing so will lead you to the product page that features more photos of the shoes from different angles. On the right side of the photos are buttons that indicate the size options available at that moment. Right below is the "Add to Cart" button so that the shopper won't have to waste time searching for a way to proceed with the purchase.

As you can see, minimizing the barriers between interest and the checkout process can be done through the right visual cues and considering which options and features should be placed near one another.

7. <u>Twitch</u>

This app has gained a large following after its pioneering ideas about providing an uninterrupted experience to its users. By enabling gamers to continue watching a stream even when they leave the app, they have set themselves apart from competitors who don't offer the same feature at the time.

Even when others caught up to their UX design, the Twitch team continued to develop new features that the gaming community truly appreciate. For example, Twitch users don't have to worry about losing the stream when they have to lock their mobile devices. The video they have been watching will still be there upon their return.

The purpose of the app is clear. They want to provide a seamless user experience without completely shutting out the real world. Because of their excellent design choices, Twitch has become the preferred streaming app even for large-scale e-sports events and competitions.

No UX design can be recognized as excellent if it doesn't consider the actual needs and wants of the users while also managing to capture and keep their attention. All of the examples given in this chapter showcase how brands and companies have successfully made the most of their brands through the implementation of the right UX design.

I hope these will inspire you to pursue your interest in this field, and perhaps one day, your designs will also encourage others to appreciate the value of an amazing UX design.

Something to Think About...

Based on what you have learned so far about UX design, do you think you have what it takes to grow and reach the top of this field?

CHAPTER 10

THE FUTURE OF UX DESIGN

Chapter 10 – The Future of UX Design

By now, you've learned what a UX designer does, as well as how companies value this field of expertise. However, what does the future hold for UX designers? If you're thinking about becoming one, wouldn't you want to know first if this is something that can be a fulfilling and exciting pursuit in life? Moreover, with the rising trend for automation, are UX designers in danger of being replaced by AI?

Let's find out more about where UX design is heading in this chapter.

> "Design creates culture. Culture shapes values. Values determine the future."
>
> -Robert L. Peters

The field of UX has reached its so-called "Golden Era" in 2010 up to 2017. During this period, the idea that user experience must be given priority has entered mainstream media. Several companies recruited UX professionals to either rebrand their business or to help in starting up new brands.

As expected, however, this once rapidly rising trend began to slow down after teams of UX designers have been hired by companies around the world. But fear not! The demand for UX designers is not going to disappear any time soon.

Why?

Because the nature of UX adapts to whatever new technology comes out next. Now that companies have realized why they should pay attention to UX, the need to have professionals on board keeps this field vibrant and enticing for many aspiring designers.

Take note that as technology develops and evolves, the expectations for UX designers also increase. That's why even professionals with several years of experience take the initiative to continually learn and stay up-to-date with trends.

What trends in UX can we anticipate for the future though?

According to experts, below are five key changes that will likely happen in the years to come:

- **Higher Demand for Specialization**

    While improving your overall knowledge and skills as a UX designer will get you a stable career, specializing in a particular area or discipline is the name of the game in the future.

    You will notice this trend starting already as some companies post job ads that are more specific about the capabilities of the UX professional they are looking for. Popular examples of UX specialists include interaction designers, content designers, and voice command specialists.

    Don't worry though because adapting a specialty is a lot easier once you already have a working background in UX design. As a beginner, however, work on acquiring the general abilities that a professional should possess. Take a diverse set of classes now to set yourself up for a more dynamic career path later on,

- **Voice Commands**

    Ever since the global pandemic stunned the world, the demand for contactless interfaces has never been higher. Touch commands, while still widely used, will gradually be overtaken by voice commands.

    To be fair, the development of voice user interfaces has long begun years ago. At the moment, the most popular ones are Apple's Siri, Amazon's Alexa, and Google Home. Still, the applications of these interfaces are mostly limited to personal, home, and work use.

    In the coming years, the use of voice commands will spread to public spaces, such as ticketing machines, elevators, and ATMs. Therefore, UX designers should start learning now how to incorporate more voice commands in their design.

    It's not only a matter of skills, however. UX designers must also study how to make voice commands more usable while remaining a secure way of interacting with products and programs. Moreover, combining voice interfaces with more traditional UX design elements should not be overlooked, especially since users will still long for the familiarity of visual feedback and animations, among others.

- **3D Interface and Virtual/Augmented Reality (VR/AR)**

    As 3D interfaces and VR/AR technology become more accessible, UX designers must also keep up and incorporate the new developments into their designs. This means utilizing more intuitive gestures and voice commands to interact with the product.

In terms of animations, UX designers must also expand their skillsets that have been honed mostly on one-dimensional spaces. They must also figure out a way to maximize the level of engagement that simulated environments have beyond their novelty to the users. For example, the AR mobile game "Pokemon Go" started with a bang that quickly died down when the development team wasn't able to keep things fresh and exciting for gamers who are not big fans of its source material.

- **Motion Design**

    More and more people find motion design as engaging and easier to use. As a result, UX designers should look into optimizing gestures such as tapping, swiping, and even tilting the entire device.

    Since motion design is more often applied to smartphones and tablets, the screen size is much smaller compared to computers. Therefore, the goal of UX designers is not just to create an interesting and useful gestural interface. They must also find a way to present all the important information without overcrowding the screen and turning off the user.

- **Artificial Intelligence**

    Working with AI is the dream of many people in the tech industry. However, some wonder if UX designers will eventually be replaced by AIs since they can also analyze historical and current data to predict how users will behave.

    The answer remains to be a resounding "No." Though AI can process large amounts of data and quickly produce good prototypes, they still can't apply true empathy and understand the nuances of being human.

Take note that the relationship between designers and AI is not a competition, to begin with. Instead, UX designers are expected to work along with AI to make the job faster and easier. AI will handle the data analysis, while the designer can take on the other approaches to data gathering, such as user interviews. Designs should also learn how to develop their designs further based on the analysis conducted by the AI.

As you can see, UX design has plenty of opportunities to offer as it continually evolves through time. In the future, it may become different from how it is known today, but that's one of the exciting parts of this field!

Becoming a UX design these days is easier than ever. Start now so you can experience the evolution of different new technologies that will likely persist through the coming years.

CHAPTER 11

PUTTING IT ALL TOGETHER

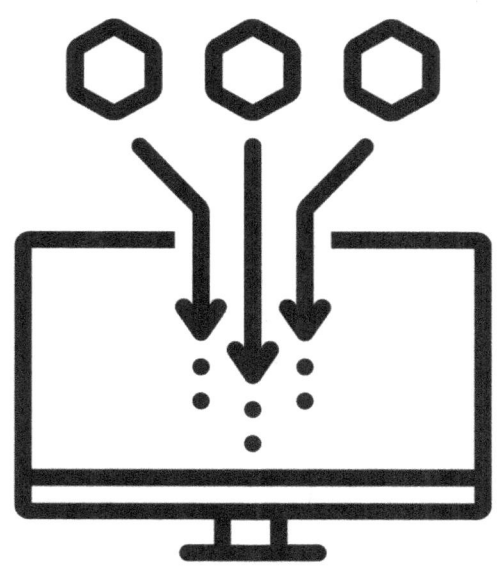

Chapter 11 – Putting It All Together

Being a UX designer is all about connecting with others on a deep level. You can't create designs that are solely based on what you like or want out of the product. Your goals should always be aligned with the needs and preferences of the users because, at the end of the day, your success depends on whether or not they find the product useful, usable, and delightful.

The six UX design principles serve as guides to professionals and companies on implementing the design theories that have been proven to be effective over the years. I hope you will take to heart each principle and make an effort to apply them in ways that will truly enhance the final product.

To help you remember these principles, let me highlight again the key takeaway points for each:

- Your design should be created with the users in mind, not just yourself.
- Quick and direct feedback must be given to users whenever required.
- Break down your content into chunks that are easier to comprehend and remember.
- Always be clear about the purpose and mechanics of your design.
- Be comfortable with using design choices that users are already familiar with—you don't have to reinvent the wheel every single time.
- Aim to delight your users through creativity, efficiency, and personal touches.

In conclusion, a career as a UX designer can be a promising path for anyone who believes in developing user-centric products that are easy to use. These professionals can tap into the minds and emotions of others and use the insights they have gained to encourage people to form a positive attachment with the product.

After everything you have learned in this book, have you decided to become a professional UX designer? If you did, your next step is to acquire the necessary skills and qualities for this career. Several online classes can be easily accessed these days—some of them are for free.

You have done well so far by taking the time to read this introductory book about UX design. Now, you've got to work on building a solid foundation to jumpstart your career in this field. I wish you the best of luck!

Enjoyed reading this book? I'd appreciate it if you would leave a review on Amazon.